Iris

Iris

Berrocal

CONTENTS

A^{LL NAMES USED IN THIS STORY ARE PSEUDONYMS}

My Grandma
   Always wishes
My Aunt
Would be different than how she is
Always wishing
My aunt would be thinner
Would be different from how she is
Each attempt closer than the last
My aunt would be thinner
Closer to her old self
My aunt, thinner
Each attempt closer than the last
Closer to her old self
Who I've heard had it together
Each attempt closer than the last
Instead of further away
I've heard she had it together
I've heard she was thriving
Further away from home
She had a job, an apartment, a life
I've heard she was thriving
I am not sure it's possible
She had a job, an apartment, a life
She doesn't work anymore
I'm not sure it's possible
My Mom says Aunt Leah has the maturity of a three year old

She doesn't work anymore
She can't hold down a job
My Mom says Aunt Leah has the maturity of a three year old
My Aunt
She can't hold down a job
My Grandma

My Aunt
    Has always been on a diet
For as long as I can remember
But still goes to In n' Out
She's always been on a diet
But always used to take me to restaurants
I hear she goes to In n' Out
And "binges"
She always used to take me to restaurants
So I could eat while she had nothing
She binges
Then goes right back on her diet
I ate while she had nothing
She'd watch me eat
She'd go right back on her diet
Another one of her cycles
She'd watch me eat
I didn't know how weird it was at the time
Another one of her cycles
She has bipolar like I do
I didn't know how weird it was at the time
Maybe she used me as an excuse to buy things?
She has bipolar like I do
But we are not the same person
Maybe she used me as an excuse to buy things?
She bought me books too

We are not the same person
Supposedly I'm more like my Uncle Liam
She bought me books too
For as long as I can remember
Supposedly I'm more like my Uncle Liam
My Aunt

When I turned fifteen or sixteen
       Mom put me on Jenny Craig
She thought I was too fat
My friends said I looked fine
Mom put me on Jenny Craig
I was one pound overweight according to the BMI
My friends said I looked fine
So what she did was legal
I was one pound overweight according to the BMI
Now, according to the BMI, I am obese
So what she did was legal
I'm pretty sure I wasn't overweight, just a normal developing girl
Now, according to the BMI, I am obese
Fuck that
I'm pretty sure I wasn't overweight, just a normal developing girl
That's what the pictures from the time show
Fuck that shit
And yet my Mom desperately wanted me to lose weight
That's what the pictures from the time show
She was afraid that if I were too fat, it would cast a shadow on my life
My Mom desperately wanted me to lose weight
The meal plans shrunk to less and less calories as I got older
She was afraid that if I were too fat, it would cast a shadow on my life
She didn't know that she was the shadow
The meal plans shrunk to less and less calories as I got older
Finally, one day, I walked out of my weekly consultation

She didn't know that she was the shadow
Finally, one day, when I was eighteen, I refused to step on the scale
Finally, one day, I walked out of my weekly consultation
She thought I was too fat
Finally, one day, when I was eighteen, I refused to step on the scale
When I turned fifteen or sixteen

There is a picture of me
    Being kissed by a dolphin
My boobs haven't grown in yet
I am long and lean
Being kissed by a dolphin
On the island of Roatan
I am long and lean
Nice and skinny
On the island of Roatan
I went to dolphin camp
Nice and skinny
I was still a kid
I went to dolphin camp
Got my junior open water dive certification
I was still a kid
With a kid's innocence
Got my junior open water dive certification
Saw the beauty of the ocean
With a kid's innocence
My Mom saw that beauty wrecked with overfishing
Saw the beauty of the ocean
Was bad at diving
My Mom saw that beauty wrecked with overfishing
That's how adults see things
Was bad at diving
But years later, Mom said, you can look like that again

That's how adults see things
I was fucking terrified
Years later, Mom said, you can look like that again
I don't want to turn back time
I was fucking terrified
She wants me to look like a kid with no boobs and no hips?
I don't want to turn back time
My boobs haven't grown in yet
She wants me to look like a kid with no boobs and no hips?
There is a picture of me
One time Levi felt particularly sorry for me
He called my situation anorexia by proxy
He said sometimes the parents of mentally ill people
Are crazier than the patients themselves
He called my situation anorexia by proxy
My Mom once yelled at me for eating a cookie
Crazier than the patient herself
She said it was just like abusing alcohol or drugs
My Mom once yelled at me for eating a cookie
I don't know how she knew, it was none of her business
She said it was just like abusing alcohol or drugs
Apparently getting angry is the answer to that?
I don't know how she knew, it was none of her business
As a church lady would tell her some time…before or later
I learned that getting angry is not the answer
So when my son abuses alcohol or drugs, I don't get angry with him
As a church lady would tell her some time…before or later
When my Mom vented what a tragedy it was that I ate too much
When my son abuses alcohol or drugs, I don't get angry with him
The church lady said that my plate is my business
When my Mom vented what a tragedy it was that I ate too much
And surely I would end up obese just like her best friend Sarah
The church lady said my plate is my business

And my fate is my own
That surely I would end up obese just like her best friend Sarah
To her most people are obese
But my fate is my own
And Americans are big
To her most people are obese
She is warped to this day
Americans are big
Is what Stepdad's cousin told her
She is warped to this day
But not as bad as she was
When Stepdad's cousin said what he said
She saw that light
She saw that light
Sometimes the parents of mentally ill people
Are crazy. But not as bad.
One time Levi felt particularly sorry for me

My Mom has a tendency to make things small
        She once said that she questions whether the Holocaust
Was really as severe as everyone says it was
And she always questions those rapes
She never questions whether the Holocaust
Happened
And she always questions those rapes
Whether they weren't between people falling in love
Happens
I guess
Whether they weren't between people falling in love
Or people who had too much to drink at a party
I guess
She's never been raped
I bet she's had too much to drink at a party
And never woke up with her pants down
She's never been raped
When Naamah told her she had been accused of rape
Mom sympathized with Naamah
Me, I told her if she ever fucked me, G-d help her
When Naamah told her she had been accused of rape
She told Mom she was afraid I might kill her
Me, I told her if she ever fucked me, G-d help her
I really would have killed her, without a moment's hesitation
She told Mom she was afraid I might kill her
Poor, poor, terrified rapist

I really would have killed her, without a moment's hesitation
And I would have been willing to take the consequences
Poor, poor, terrified rapist
Was really as severe as everyone says it was
And I would have been willing to take the consequences
My Mom has a tendency to make things small

My Grandma says Leah is "unlovely"
    I think that's a terrible thing to say
About your own daughter
But part of me doesn't really blame her
It's a terrible thing to say
When your child is yelling at you
But part of me doesn't really blame her
Quietly sarcastic things
When your child is yelling at you
Has yelled at you for years
Quietly sarcastic things
Can be your only weapon
Yelling for years
Mom says they should go to therapy
Your only weapon
That the relationship is unhealthy
Mom says they should go to therapy
I genuinely believe my Mom is right
The relationship is unhealthy
Not just because she says so
I genuinely believe my Mom is right
Leah has ranted at Grandma for years
They fight over money
Not just because she says so
Leah has ranted at Grandma for years
Why don't you ever love me

Just because she says so
She gets everything she wants
Why don't you ever love me
Your own daughter
She gets everything she wants
My Grandma says Leah is "unlovely"
Grandma says
Her mother didn't really like her
She has a memory
Of her mother holding her sister
Her mother didn't really like her
If Barbies had existed back then
Her mother holding her sister
Grandma wished she would have held her too
If Barbies had existed back then
Grandma would have gotten the Ken doll
Grandma wished her Mom would have held her too
But she didn't
Grandma would have gotten the Ken doll
She was kind of the "black sheep"
Grandma's Mom didn't hold her that day
Many years later, my Grandpa would call my Mom that
She was kind of the "black sheep"
Now, many years later
Many years later, my Grandpa would call my Mom that
But in the present, my Grandma is continuing the cycle
Now, many years later
My Grandma calls Leah unlovely
My Grandma is continuing the cycle
She can't see through it
My Grandma calls Leah unlovely
And can't accept that she's not a mature person
She can't see through it

Hoping she'll lose weight and be back to her old self
She can't accept that she's not a mature person
And what you were, you can't be anymore
Hoping she'll lose weight and be back to her old self
It's a vicious relationship
What you were, you can't be anymore
She has a memory
It's a vicious relationship
Grandma says
My Grandma had a boyfriend from Europe
She adored him
She introduced him to her family
And he promptly left her
She adored him
She was truly in love
He promptly left her
Once he saw the shitshow that was her family
She was truly in love
But in Europe they think of it as more "marrying into a family"
Once he saw the shitshow that was her family
He didn't think it was up to par
In Europe they think of it as more "marrying into a family"
I wonder if you would have taken one look at my family and ran
He didn't think it was up to par
I wonder if you would have thought we were up to par
I wonder if you would have taken one look at my family and ran
Just like my Grandma's ex-boyfriend did
I wonder if you would have thought we were up to par
I wonder if I would have thought your family was up to par
Family mattered to my Grandma's ex-boyfriend
Silly things matter to my Grandma today
I wonder if I would have liked your family

She says today that a person should always marry someone as similar
to them as possible
Silly things matter to my Grandma today
Like being of the same age, culture, and things like that
She says today that a person should always marry someone as similar
to them as possible
I think that's a sad mentality
The same age? The same culture?
Where's the fun in that?
I think that's a sad mentality
Sure, it's easier, but you never really grow
Where's the fun in that?
She introduced him to her family
Sure, it's easier, but you never really grow
My Grandma had a boyfriend from Europe

G randma ended up marrying my Grandpa, Jett
  A man ten years her senior
Who hit her one occasion (maybe more)
And who was very introverted
A man ten years her senior
So they had no cultural references in common
Who was very introverted
So he never wanted to go places with Grandma, hang with her and
her friends
They had no cultural references in common
There wasn't a sense of going through life together
He never wanted to go places with Grandma, hang with her friends
When they went to Venice he just wanted to stay in and read
There wasn't a sense of going through life together
There were no references in common, period
When they went to Venice he just wanted to stay in and read
He ended up cheating on her with his receptionist
There were no references in common, period
He loved to ski, she didn't like to ski
He ended up cheating on her with his receptionist
Got a vasectomy on her demand
He loved to ski, she didn't like to ski
He loved piano, she didn't
Got a vasectomy on her demand
When his second wife wanted kids he couldn't have them
He loved piano, she didn't

Once she left him, she went to ball games with her boyfriend, Elijah
When his second wife wanted kids he couldn't have them
He left nothing to his kids in his will
Once she left him, she went to ball games with her boyfriend, Elijah
Who hit her one occasion (maybe more)
He left nothing to his kids in his will
Grandma ended up marrying my Grandpa, Jett

Mom says Jett was basically a good person
She says Grandma was upset about the age gap
Between them
So she exaggerates stuff to justify her upset
She says Grandma was upset about the age gap
Although if he hit her, being upset is justified
So she exaggerates stuff to justify her upset
These days she goes on and on about how age gaps in relationships
are bad
If he hit her, being upset is justified
And Jett wasn't a good person after all
These days she goes on and on about how age gaps in relationship
are bad
Which bothers me because I skew both young and old
Jett was not a good person if he hit my Grandma
And I am sick of Mom defending him
I skew both young and old
I would never hit a partner who was younger than me
I am sick of Mom defending him
I am sick of Mom not believing my Grandma
I would never hit a partner who was younger than me
Or older for that matter
I am sick of Mom not believing my Grandma
I am sick of Mom not believing me!
I would never hit a partner who was older than me
There needs to be equality in age gap relationships, though

I am sick of Mom not believing me!
I am sick of Mom not believing anyone
There needs to be equality in age gap relationships
The older partner needs to respect the younger partner
I am sick of Mom not believing anyone
Between them
The older partner needs to respect the younger partner
Mom says Jett was basically a good person

I think it was after the divorce
    Jett took the kids
On a trip to Europe
To make them like him
Jett took the kids,
Mom, Leah, Aaron, and Liam
On a trip to Europe
To see the world
Mom, Leah, Aaron, and Liam
Four kids in Europe
Seeing the world for the first time
Growing to like their father
Four kids in Europe
Many years later
Growing to like their father
My Grandma shakes her head in dismay
Many years later
Mom still feels loyalty to Jett
My Grandma shakes her head in dismay
At how well that ploy worked
Mom still feels loyalty to Jett
I am not sure why, but kids don't always see the whole picture
That ploy worked really well
Mom defends Jett to this day
I am not sure why, but kids don't always see the whole picture
They just see a trip to Europe

Mom defends Jett to this day
She loves her father
They just see a trip to Europe
On a trip to Europe
She loves her father
I think it was after the divorce

After Grandma divorced Jett
    She found the love of her life, Elijah
Same age, extroverted
A kind soul who loved animals and voted Republican
She found the love of her life, Elijah
A man who would be her boyfriend for the rest of his life
A kind soul who loved animals and voted Republican
My Grandma being a socialist and all...
A man who would be her boyfriend for the rest of his life
He would die of lung cancer when I was around five
My Grandma was a socialist
But that didn't matter
He would die of lung cancer when I was around five
I think my Grandma cared for him in his last days
It didn't matter
That they never married
I think my Grandma cared for him in his last days
She kept a picture of him until she moved into our house
They never married
But he was the real love of her life
She kept a picture of him until she moved into our house
He wore a drivers' cap in the photo
He was the real love of her life
They went to ball games together
He wore a drivers' cap in the photo
Looked straight into the camera and smiled

They went to ball games together
They were both extroverts
Looked straight into the camera and smiled
Same age, extroverted
They were both extroverts
After Grandma divorced Jett

Jett wouldn't even hire someone
    To help take care of the kids
While Grandma was studying
To be a lawyer
To help take care of the kids
He said we can do that once you start making money
At being a lawyer
Missing the point entirely
Once you start making money
We can start caring for Leah properly
Missing the point entirely
Leaving Leah alone
We can start caring for Leah properly
When she's not alone after school
Leaving Leah alone
Fuck, even the babysitter molested her
When she's not alone after school
Just a kid
Fuck, even the babysitter molested her
No one deserves that
Just a kid
Having terrifying audio and visual hallucinations
Like bugs crawling on her skin and G-d knows what else
No one deserves that
Having terrifying audio and visual hallucinations
I remember what that was like

No one deserves that
I wouldn't wish it on my worst enemy
I remember what that was like
While Grandma was studying
I wouldn't wish it on my worst enemy
Jett wouldn't even hire someone

One time
        My Grandma came to change it
The baby's diaper
Uncle Liam's diaper
My Grandma came to change it
Her first born son's diaper
Uncle Liam's diaper
And she saw a handprint
Her first born son's diaper
Her beloved son
And she saw a handprint
And knew what had happened
Her beloved son
Her pride and joy
She knew what had happened
And it broke her heart
Her pride and joy
Many years later
It broke her heart
That same pain in her eyes
Many years later
"You don't hit a baby!"
That same pain in her eyes
That same horror on her face
"You don't hit a baby!"
As she sits in her office chair

That same horror on her face
As we sit in her office together
As she sits in her office chair
The baby's diaper
As we sit in her office together
One time

One time Grandma was talking to me
In a very loving, sweet way
Leah was around
She said why don't you talk to me like that
In a very loving, sweet way
Leah wasn't angry
She said why don't you talk to me like that
It was more sad than anything else
Leah wasn't angry
I was a young teenager
It was more sad than anything else
A silent wishing for affection
I was a young teenager
Really, I'm not sure how old I was
A silent wishing for affection
Honestly, as a teenager, I didn't get that much affection either
I'm not sure how old I was
My memory is creaky
Honestly, as a teenager, I didn't get that much affection either
It was just do your schoolwork
My memory is creaky
But I remember some things
It was just do your schoolwork
I remember that
I remember some things
I don't remember the emotions

But I remember the emotions were there
Like a bookmark I remember that
I don't remember the emotions
Leah was around
Like a bookmark I remember that
One time Grandma was talking to me

My Mom was always the black sheep of her family
     She smoked and drank
Was into radical politics
Literally my granddad called her "the black sheep" once
She smoked and drank
I have never done either
Literally my granddad called her "the black sheep" once
I imagine she had a hard time fitting in with the rest of the family
I have never done either
Esther once referred to me as "straight edge"
I imagine she had a hard time fitting in with the rest of the family
Introverted Liam, Aaron who went to boarding school, bipolar Leah
Esther once referred to me as "straight edge"
Sounds cooler than saying you are sober
Introverted Liam, Aaron who went to boarding school, bipolar Leah
It sounds like everyone had their own thing going on
Sounds cooler than saying you are sober
So thank you Esther
It sounds like everyone had their own thing going on
Everyone has their own lives
So thank you Esther
Now I can be cool
Everyone has their own lives
But grown up, most of them live in the same neighborhood
Now I can be cool
I'm not sure my Mom could have been, back then

Grown up, most of them live in the same neighborhood
Family dynamics
I'm not sure my Mom could have been, back then
She was into radical politics
Family dynamics
My Mom was always the black sheep of her family

Where does Uncle Aaron fit in?
He wants nothing to do with this dynamic
He speaks to Grandma
But he barely speaks to Leah
He wants nothing to do with this dynamic
He lives in Berkeley
He barely speaks to Leah
Helping manage life from afar
He lives in Berkeley
In a beautiful big house
Helping manage life from afar
Stepping in more as Grandma gets older
In a beautiful big house
With a beautiful big library
Stepping in more as Grandma gets older
When Grandma is gone he will probably manage things
With a beautiful big library
I read a bit every time I go there
When Grandma is gone he will probably manage things
The only problem is his common-law wife, Abigail
I read a bit every time I go there
He has many books I've read before and many I haven't
The only problem is his common-law wife, Abigail
She thinks she knows how other people should live
He has many books I've read before, and many I haven't

He has The Book Thief, some manga, Precious, vegan cookbooks, and Eat Pray Love
She thinks she knows how other people should live
She thinks my Mom should get a job
He has The Book Thief, some manga, Precious, vegan cookbooks, and Eat Pray Love
He speaks to Grandma
She thinks my Mom should get a job
Where does Uncle Aaron fit in?

You could say that Aunt Abigail is a shitty person
        Or you could say that she is very materialistic
My Mom says
She is very traditional
You could say she is very materialistic
When I told her about Solomon and Asher
She is very traditional
She asked if Solomon had a job
When I told her about Solomon and Asher
It was implied I was trying to decide between the two
She asked if Solomon had a job
I said he was disabled
It was implied I was trying to decide between the two
In all fairness, she might not have known Asher was a bit old for me
I said he was disabled
And then I said Asher was a millionaire
In all fairness, she might not have known Asher was a bit old for me
We did like each other
When I said Asher was a millionaire
She said well go with that then
Asher and I did like each other
We once went to Fashion Island
She said well go with that then
Because he had more money
We once went to Fashion Island
Late at night, when all the shops were closed

He had money
But he never spent a lot on me
Late at night, when all the shops were closed
My Mom says
But he never spent a lot on me
You could say that Aunt Abigail is a shitty person

Where does Uncle Liam fit in?
He has bipolar as well
And most likely autism
Like me
He has bipolar as well
But isn't like Leah
People say he is more like me
We are both pretty calm people
He isn't like Leah
Who is always emotionally all over the place
We are both pretty calm people
My family didn't initially believe my diagnosis
She's always emotionally all over the place
The stereotypical bipolar person
My family didn't initially believe my diagnosis
Because I am not like that
The stereotypical bipolar person
Grandma says she is off the charts, severe bipolar
Because I am not like that
But Mom and Noah think she probably has something else too
Grandma says she is off the charts, severe bipolar
But there may be more to the story
Mom and Noah think she probably has something else too
Mom thinks it may be autism
There may be more to the story
As to why Leah acts how she acts

Mom thinks it may be autism
I think it may be SOMETHING
Why Leah acts how she acts
Most likely autism
I think it may be SOMETHING
Where does Uncle Liam fit in?

I also have a cousin named Colette
    We used to be close
    Until my teenage years
    When I started acting sort of obnoxious
    We used to be close
    Leah tried to spoil her once too
    When I started acting sort of obnoxious
    Colette said she could tell Leah didn't have the money to buy her lots
of stuff
    Leah tried to spoil her once too
    Colette is her niece too, after all
    Colette said she could tell Leah didn't have the money to buy her lots
of stuff
    That made it awkward for her
    Colette is her niece too, after all
    Once she was upset that she couldn't get her hair done, all pretty, like
me
    That made it awkward for her
    Maybe?
    Once she was upset that she couldn't get her hair done, all pretty, like
me
    I was always the hairdresser's favorite
    Maybe?
    I'm not really sure what was going on there
    I was always the hairdresser's favorite
    The last time I saw her, she was doing my hair for Queer Prom

I'm not really sure she knew what was going down
But if she knew, she was accepting
The last time I saw her, she was doing my hair for Queer Prom
She always loved to use my hair to experiment with new styles
If she knew, she was accepting
With my rainbow skirt
She always loved to use my hair to experiment with new styles
Until my teenage years
WIth my rainbow skirt
I also have a cousin named Colette

My Grandma
     Gives my Aunt
Everything she wants
Or every material thing
Giving my Aunt
Whatever she asks for
Every material thing
She couldn't give her safety or love
Whatever she asks for
Like to record an album with Noah
She couldn't give her safety or love
She couldn't keep her from being abused
Recording an album with Noah
Grandma hoped she could become known
Not knowing
It's a lot like self published writing
Grandma hoped she could become known
My Aunt hoped to make a little money
It's a lot like self published writing
You don't do it for the money
My Aunt hoped to make a little money
When I heard I winced
You don't do it for the money
You do it for the passion
When I heard I winced
Like every time my Aunt goes off on my Grandma

You do it for the passion
I guess like when my Aunt says why didn't you ever love me
Like every time my aunt goes off on my Grandma
Everything she wants
I guess like when my Aunt says why didn't you ever love me
My Grandma

Leah was abused
     I'm not supposed to know this
But I do
She has been raped and molested
I'm not supposed to know this
No one ever told me
She has been raped and molested
The first time when she was a small child
No one ever told me
Well, my Mom mentioned it once
The first time when she was a small child
I think she was in the shower
My Mom mentioned it once
She said how can you call it rape when you're crawling into bed with someone
I think she was in the shower though
The shower thing happened when she was young
She said how can you call it rape when you're crawling into bed with someone
I thought what if you just want cuddles
The shower thing happened when she was young
I was young when I heard
I thought what if you just want cuddles
It really pissed me off
I was young when I heard
Maybe about fifth grade or so

It really pissed me off

When I heard her molester had never been prosecuted

My Grandma told her Mom

I was older when I found out about that part

Her molester was never prosecuted

My Grandma never took him to court

I was older when I found out about that part

My Grandma didn't want Leah to be cross-examined, so she never got justice

My Grandma never took him to court

Now she gets everything she wants

My Grandma didn't want Leah to be cross-examined, so she never got justice

Now she ruins the family finances with Grandma's guilt

My Grandma once said
        Leah was once in an institution
She bought her a red robe
And Leah showed it off
Leah was once in an institution
And wasn't constantly asking for money
Leah showed it off
And was happy with what she had
She wasn't constantly asking for money
Always yelling at my Grandma
And was happy with what she had
Nowadays she never seems to have enough
Always yelling at my Grandma
And my Grandma saying cutting things back
She never seems to have enough
Grandma gets quieter as Leah gets louder
My Grandma says cutting things back
Mom says it's the cruelest thing
Grandma gets quieter as Leah gets louder
That's how she deals with the yelling
Mom says it's the cruelest thing
That Leah was once the sweetest little girl
That's how she deals with the yelling
I think Mom still sees that sweet little girl
Leah was once the sweetest little girl
Mom wanted Leah to live with her

I think Mom still sees that sweet little girl
But Grandma thought she was perfectly capable of caring for Leah
by herself
Mom wanted Leah to live with her
She bought her a red robe
But Grandma thought she was perfectly capable of caring for Leah
by herself
My Grandma once said

My Mom wanted Leah to come stay
    With her while she went to school
Mom loved Leah and didn't want her to be alone
She thought she could provide a good home
While Mom went to school
Most people break away from their families
But she thought she could provide a good home
And she could see her little sister needed her
Most people break away from their families
I know I have to a degree
She could see her little sister needed her
So she begged and begged
I know I have to a degree
Although I still text Mom every day
She begged and begged
But Grandma said no
I text Mom every day
Even though I am in college now
Grandma said no
She thought she could raise Leah fine on her own
I am in college now
I try to be there for the people who need me
She thought she could raise Leah on her own
As a full time Law student
I try to be there for the people who need me
Although nothing on par with my Mom

As a full time Law student

Wait...what? I am a more-than-part-time-less-than-full-time journalism student!

Nothing on par with my Mom

Mom loved Leah and didn't want her to be alone

Wait...what? I am a more-than-part-time-less-than-full-time journalism student!

My Mom wanted Leah to come stay

My aunt tends
      To yell at Grandma
When she doesn't give her
Something she wants
When she yells at Grandma
It scares Grandma
So she gives her what she wants
Mom says Grandma needs to stand up for herself
It scares Grandma
It scares me too
Mom says Grandma needs to stand up for herself
But that's hard to do
It scares me too
It's one of the reasons I left
It's hard to do
Being afraid she'd be angry
It's one of the reasons I left
I just plain like Grandma better
Being afraid she'd be angry
With Grandma I'm not scared I'm walking on eggshells
I just plain like Grandma better
Not that Leah isn't nice
With Grandma I'm not scared I'm walking on eggshells
Scared of making her angry
Not that Leah isn't nice
Playing board games and reading books with her can be fun

But I'm scared of making her angry
Which was why I sometimes gave her time I didn't want to give
Playing board games and reading books with her can be fun
When she doesn't give
I sometimes gave her time I didn't want to give
My aunt tends

One time my Mom gave my aunt a pillow
    It was embroidered with the words "Never Grow Up"
She hoped my aunt would see it and know
It was ok to be herself
It was embroidered with the words "Never Grow Up"
Noah says my Aunt isn't really an adult
It's ok to be yourself
He said my aunt had no sense of money
Noah says my Aunt isn't really an adult
It's just kind of the air she gives off
He said my aunt had no sense of money
I know her, she spends it like water
It's just the kind of air she gives off
My Mom says my Aunt is like a little girl
I know her, she spends money like water
That it's cruel to expect her to act like an adult
My Mom says my aunt is like a little girl
Apparently some psychiatrist said she has the maturity of a three-year-old
It's cruel to expect her to act like an adult
And she will never change in that regard
Apparently some psychiatrist said she has the maturity of a three-year-old
My Grandma is trying to teach her to manage her money
And she will never change in that regard
Where her maturity is concerned

My Grandma is trying to teach her to manage her money
Learning to manage money at, what, forty? Fifty?
Where her maturity is concerned
If she doesn't know by now I don't think she'll ever learn
Learning to manage money at, what, forty? Fifty?
She hoped my aunt would see it and know
If she doesn't know by now I don't think she'll ever learn
One time my Mom gave my aunt a pillow

26

When I stopped seeing Leah
      I kept seeing Grandma
Sometimes I would arrive at Grandma's house
When Leah was there
I kept seeing Grandma
I wasn't in the mood to cut off my entire family yet
When Leah was there
Her jealousy made things awkward
I wasn't in the mood to cut off my entire family yet
My Grandma and I were still close in those days
Leah's jealousy made things awkward
Leah would often yell at me because she was jealous
My Grandma and I were still close in those days
Oddly enough, that would never really be tested
Leah would often yell at me because she was jealous
Wishing I was hanging out with her instead
Oddly enough, that would never be tested
Although one could argue that Grandma wasn't sugar and cream to
me either
Wishing I was hanging out with her instead
I didn't like her volatile moods
One could argue that Grandma wasn't sugar and cream to me either
I still remember her lecturing me on why going to school is a good
idea
I didn't like Leah's volatile moods
But I didn't like that sort of treatment either

I still remember her lecturing me on why going to school is a good
idea
    What a thing to say to a wannabe homeschooler
    I didn't like that sort of treatment either
    But I never cut her off
    What a thing to say to a wannabe homeschooler
    Sometimes I would arrive at Grandma's house
    But I never cut her off
    When I stopped seeing Leah

27

L eah, incidentally, did spoil me
	But I left her anyway
Preferring Grandma's quieter company
And just her as a person
I left her anyway
Leah took me to restaurants, bought me books
Just her as a person
Took me on walks with her dogs, played board games with me
Leah took me to restaurants, bought me books
I think she bought me FIRESTAR'S QUEST
Took me on walks with her dogs, played board games with me
She introduced me to CHICKEN SOUP FOR THE SOUL
I think she bought me FIRESTAR'S QUEST
She had all the Shiloh books too
She introduced me to CHICKEN SOUP FOR THE SOUL
I also read PETSPEAK at her house
She had all the Shiloh books too
I don't think I read them all
I also read PETSPEAK at her house
That one had a step-by-step guide to training cats
I don't think I read them all
I was too young for NIGHT FALLS FAST
PETSPEAK had a step-by-step guide to training cats
She also had Vogue on her square glass coffee table
I was too young for NIGHT FALLS FAST
Too young to read about suicide

She also had Vogue on her square glass coffee table
I just never picked it up
Too young to read about suicide
Preferring Grandma's quieter company
I just never picked it up
Leah, incidentally, did spoil me

28

L eah did forgive me
It did stop
She saw I was depressed
Which my Mom did not
It did stop
She stopped yelling at me every time she saw me
My Mom did not
Stop...well...insisting I go to an independent study that was killing me
She stopped yelling at me every time she saw me
She saw something was going on
Mom didn't stop insisting I go to an independent study that was killing me
At the time, school was my kryptonite
She saw something was going on
A certain insight my mother lacked
At the time, school was my kryptonite
But my Mom didn't know that
A certain insight my mother lacked
Rev Angel saw I was depressed too
My Mom didn't know that
"What happened?" Rev Angel asked
Rev Angel saw I was depressed too
She asked that question over a slice of cake
"What happened?" Rev Angel asked
How many times can a heart break?

She asked that question over a slice of cake
Sometimes people would see straight through me
How many times can a heart break?
She offered spiritual counseling, I didn't know how to say yes
Sometimes people would see straight through me
She saw I was depressed
She offered spiritual counseling, I didn't know how to say yes
Leah did forgive me

29

Mom says Leah is like a little girl
There is some truth to this
Noah notices it too
But Grandma won't acknowledge it
There is some truth to this
When buying things, Leah never looks at the price tag
Grandma won't acknowledge it
She believes Leah can change
When buying things, Leah never looks at the price tag
I swear she used to use me as an excuse to spend money
She believes Leah can change
And stop her from engaging in her favorite hobby of all
I swear she used to use me as an excuse to spend money
Always buying things for me
Spending money: her favorite hobby of all
We used to go to restaurants almost every meal; didn't want me eating her diet food
Always buying things for me
Like books
We used to go to restaurants almost every meal; didn't want me eating her diet food
I liked IHOP
Books
I remember Chicken Soup for the Soul in particular
I liked IHOP
Especially their pumpkin pancakes

I remember Chicken Soup for the Soul in particular
I even tried writing for them once
Pumpkin pancakes
So decadent
I even tried writing for them once
Noah notices it too
So decadent
Mom says Leah is like a little girl

30

I remember
     Hiding in a closet
In the Green room
Listening
Hiding in a closet
ARE YOU GONNA WAIT UNTIL I DO SOMETHING TO YOU?
LIstening
And peering through the slats at the mirror
ARE YOU GONNA WAIT UNTIL I DO SOMETHING TO YOU?
My aunt yelling at my Grandma
Peering through the slats in the mirror
I cannot see myself
My aunt yelling at my Grandma
It is seldom this bad
I cannot see myself
Only the closet
It is seldom this bad
My aunt has been violent in the past
But I seldom have to hide in the closet
Peering outside, looking at the green couch
My aunt has been violent in the past
In the future she would chase me around the dining room table
Peering outside, looking at the green couch
Luckily in the future she has a bad foot

In the future, she would chase me around the dining room table
I'LL RING YOUR BELL!
Luckily in the future she has a bad foot
In that future I go outside and hide in some shrubbery
I'LL RING YOUR BELL!
In the Green Room
In that future I go outside and hide in some shrubbery
I remember

31

My Dad and I
Never got along
He was always touching me
I never liked it
We never got along
He would always call me
I never liked it
I always dreaded the calls
He would always call me
Crying, saying he missed me, wanted me to come visit him in Cartagena
I always dreaded the calls
Once he put cousin Valerie on the line, and she asked me why I never came to Cartagena
Crying, saying he missed me, wanted me to come visit him in Cartagena
Always made me feel really guilty and crappy
Once he put cousin Valerie on the line, and she asked me why I never came to Cartagena
Even then I thought that was sort of low
Always made me feel really guilty and crappy
Made me not want to visit him in Cartagena
Even then I thought that was sort of low
Always trying to make me feel guilty
Made me not want to visit him in Cartagena
When I finally did, he wouldn't stop touching me

Always trying to make me feel guilty
It wasn't sexual touching, but it did feel weird
When I finally did, he wouldn't stop touching me
I wasn't allowed more than about a yard from him at any given time
It wasn't sexual touching, but it did feel weird
All those damp smooches
I wasn't allowed more than about a yard from him at any given time
He was always touching me
All those damp smooches
My Dad and I

32

My biological Dad used to touch me a lot
It was never sexual
But it bothered me a great deal
Nonetheless
It was never sexual
My Dad never molested me
Nonetheless
It was still gross and unpleasant
My Dad never molested me
So sometimes it's hard to explain to people
How that can be
Can't I just let it go?
Sometimes it's hard to explain to people
That he never touched by chest, or my butt
Can't I just let it go
That he touched me constantly?
He never touched my chest, or my butt
Thank G-d
He touched me constantly
Never letting me more than a yard away from him
Thank G-d
Things never turned sexual
He never let me more than a yard away from him
It still felt gross
Things never turned sexual
It wasn't motivated by that

It still felt gross
I still felt sort of violated
It wasn't motivated by sexuality
It bothered me a great deal
I still felt sort of violated
My biological Dad used to touch me a lot

My bioDad didn't know
That I was being homeschooled
He would have been dismayed
If he had known
I was being homeschooled
Mom said, "Alexandra, just tell him you go to a small school with lots
of friends."
If he had known
He would have wanted me to go to school
Mom said, "Alexandra, just tell him you go to a small school with lots
of friends."
I complied. I didn't mind lying to him.
He would have wanted me to go to school
He would have worried about me having friends
I complied. I didn't mind lying to him.
I didn't want trouble.
He would have worried about me having friends
The last thing on my mind
I didn't want trouble
I didn't want him to fuss
The last thing on my mind
Was whether I would have friends
I didn't want him to fuss
I didn't want him to ruin this
I had friends as a homeschooler
And I wanted to be homeschooled more than anything

I didn't want him to ruin this
I didn't want him to demand that I go to school
I wanted to be homeschooled more than anything
I knew my Dad wouldn't understand
I didn't want him to demand that I go to school
He would have been dismayed
I knew my Dad wouldn't understand
My bioDad didn't know

Stepdad wanted me to be normal
       So when I suffered
He thought that was normal
And showed no sympathy
When I suffered
I was just a rebellious teenager
He showed no sympathy
Maybe he loved my Mom more
I was just a rebellious teenager
Going through rebellious teenage paces
Maybe he loved my Mom more
I don't know
Going through rebellious teenage paces
Like...being sad?
I don't know
I didn't really rebel in the conventional sense
Like...being sad?
I didn't even express that very much
I didn't really rebel in the conventional sense
Very few people knew I was sad
I didn't even express that very much
I got used to not really expressing my emotions
Very few people knew I was sad
Abel, Samuel, Esther
I got used to not really expressing my emotions
I knew it would lead me nowhere

Abel, Samuel, Esther
So I lived in quiet despair
I knew it would lead me nowhere
He thought that was normal
So I lived in quiet despair
Stepdad wanted me to be normal
During those years
My relationship with my Stepdad became rather combative
I don't regret it
It was one of the few joys I had
My relationship with my Stepdad became rather combative
I'd provoke him, he'd retaliate by hitting me (not too hard)
It was one of the few joys I had
It really annoyed my Mom
I'd provoke him, he'd retaliate by hitting me (not too hard)
He said he was training me to be a good little masochist
It really annoyed my Mom
My friend (at the time) Peter thought it was creepy
He said he was training me to be a good little masochist
He doesn't really say that anymore
My friend (at the time) Peter thought it was creepy
Looking at it like this, now, it is creepy
He doesn't really say that anymore
Although our relationship hasn't changed
Looking at it like this, now, it is creepy
But also a ton of fun!
Although our relationship hasn't changed
Well, I mean, it sort of has, I've grown up
It's been fun!
But time hasn't stopped him from stating what he thinks I should
have done, what I should do
I've grown up

But he still thinks I should have gone to public school, and that I should get a job

Time hasn't stopped him from stating what he thinks I should have done, what I should do

And it's always something I'm not quite ready for, or just plain don't want

He still thinks I should have gone to public school, and that I should get a job

I don't regret it

And it's always something I'm not quite ready for, or just plain don't want

During those years

35

If you look up pictures of Kurt Cobain, he is always smiling
    If you look up pictures of Marilyn Monroe, she is always smiling
This is what depression looks like
As often as not, it's pretending to be ok when you're not
If you look up pictures of Marilyn Monroe, she is always smiling
Even though she is carrying a mountain on her shoulders
She makes it look easy
So people think depression is easy
She is carrying a mountain on her shoulders
Obviously I wasn't as screwed-up as she was
But people think depression is easy
Or if you have "good days" where you enjoy things, the depression
isn't that bad
    I wasn't as screwed up as she was
    But I know what it's like to smile
So they said I had "good days" where I enjoyed things
And I don't deny it, I did
I know what it's like to smile
And be holding a wolf by the ears
I had good days
But the depression was still bad
I was holding a wolf by the ears
It was hard to hold, but I didn't know how to let go
The depression was bad even though I had good days
I just wore a happy mask
It was hard to hold, but I didn't know how to let go

I guess telling someone would have been letting go?
I just wore a happy mask
Pretending everything was ok when it wasn't
I guess telling someone would have been letting go?
This is what depression looks like
Pretending everything was ok when it wasn't
If you look up pictures of Kurt Cobain, he is always smiling

36

I feel like a bad daughter writing this stuff
        Revealing the secrets of my family
Things no one is supposed to tell
They'd die of shame if they knew
Revealing the secrets of my family
Revealing the secrets of family members
They'd die of shame if they knew
No one looks good here
Revealing the secrets of family members
Admittedly, some of them have a right to their secrets
No one looks good here
Not even the best of us
Admittedly, some of them have a right to their secrets
My poor Aunt Leah has been through a lot
But even the best of us
May have done bad things
My poor Aunt Leah has been through a lot
But even she has yelled at my Grandma
She's done bad things
She is not 100% innocent
Even she has yelled at my Grandma
Saying terrible things that there is no excuse for
She is not 100% innocent
Sometimes even victims have victims
Saying terrible things that there is no excuse for

Like ARE YOU GONNA WAIT UNTIL I DO SOMETHING
TO YOU
Sometimes even victims have victims
And that was a literal call for violence
Like ARE YOU GONNA WAIT UNTIL I DO SOMETHING
TO YOU
Things no one is supposed to tell
And that was a literal call for violence
I feel like a bad daughter writing this stuff

37

There are two aspects to this that are really fucked up, or have caused problems

One is that my Mom thinks Sarah is aroace (probably because she is fat)

Two is that my Mom thought Hannah was too fat to fuck me, or want to

And that made her not plan for things she should have planned for

One is that my Mom thinks Sarah is aroace (probably because she is fat)

I once heard her say, "No, Sarah doesn't like people in that way"

And that made her not plan for things she should have planned for

In reality I have talked about attraction with Sarah, and as far as I can tell she is bisexual

I once heard her say, "No, Sarah doesn't like people in that way"

And my blood boiled because I was sure she was saying it because of her weight

In reality I have talked about attraction with Sarah, and as far as I can tell she is bisexual

Although, to be fair, Sarah really doesn't like labels

And my blood boiled because I was sure she was saying it because of her weight

People who are disabled are often desexualized, and Sarah sometimes uses a wheelchair

Sarah really doesn't like labels

Because what if you want to go outside of that label?

People who are disabled are often desexualized, and Sarah sometimes uses a wheelchair

I think my Mom desexualizes fat people too

Because what if you want to go outside of that label?

What if you didn't assume things about a person based on their weight?

I think my Mom desexualizes fat people too

She didn't comprehend that I could have a sexual relationship with Hannah

What if you didn't assume things about a person based on their weight?

So in some ways, she failed to protect me, because she didn't plan for that

She didn't comprehend that I could have a sexual relationship with Hannah

"But he was too fat!" my Mom exclaimed when she found out

So in some ways, she failed to protect me, because she didn't plan for that

She naively assumed that me hanging out in Hannah's bedroom with the door shut led to...nothing

"But he was too fat!" my Mom exclaimed when she found out

Two is that my Mom thought Hannah was too fat to fuck me, or want to

She naively assumed that me hanging out in Hannah's bedroom with the door shut led to...nothing

There are two aspects to this that are really fucked up, or have caused problems

38

Part of the reason I wore a tichel for so long
Is because tichels are about not judging other people for their outward appearance
So it was a fuck you
To the fat-phobia of my family
Tichels are about not judging other people for their outward appearance
Although some may judge for the length of their skirt
The fat-phobia of my family
They were initially afraid I'd be judged for my decision
Some may judge for the length of their skirt
To some people, tichels are about slut-shaming
They were initially afraid I'd be judged for my decision
But tichels shouldn't be about that, at their best
To some people, tichels are about slut-shaming
Entire cultures submit to this mentality
But tichels shouldn't be about that, at their best
They should be a reminder that appearances don't matter
Entire cultures submit to this mentality
It's part of this thing called patriarchy
Tichels should be a reminder that appearances don't matter
Patriarchy perverts this
It's part of this thing called patriarchy
Some people say it doesn't exist
Patriarchy perverts this
It's like a bad bass line

Some people say it doesn't exist
It seems so normal to some people that they think it's normal
It's like a bad bass line
We could make a better bass line
It seems so normal to some people that they think it's normal
It is a fuck you
We could make a better bass line
Part of the reason I wore a tichel for so long

Last night, I dreamed I was marrying my first love, Iris. I wasn't terribly excited about this. I have fallen in love many times, let me assure you, and even though Iris was my first love, she wasn't my most exciting one. There are other people I'd rather marry. So I wasn't terribly excited about this. However, I was happy. I felt that it made a certain sense that things should turn out this way. It made sense that, since she was my first love, that she should also be my last. In the dream, she said I was her only friend. We were so caught up in the minutiae of the ceremony that we never actually married, but hey, that's life. And we were happy.

INTRO

So I am a goy. To be more exact, I am a shiksa. I try not to eat pork, so I am kosher in that respect, but I do love shellfish and I mix milk and meat in the same meal all the time, so in that respect, I'm really not kosher. Some people say I have the air of a baleboosteh, like my former friend Ashley and Palm Springs Alex. In other words, I have a dom air, or an air of being in charge. The last song I heard before leaving for Durango, Colorado was called "Shalom Aleichem". It would turn out to be an omen, a rough omen, but a good one. It would involve many auditory hallucinations, but life would change for the better. I would become a meshuggeneh, or a crazy person, and get a Bipolar 1 diagnosis. Many people would say that was a curse from Gott (G-d), but I sort of think it is a blessing. However, it does mean that if civilization ever collapsed, I'd be one of the first to die. I don't think about that much, but I do think about it. My ex girlfriend said she'd shoot me if that ever happened, so I wouldn't have to suffer. It's kind of her. I try to dress with tznius in mind, too. I'd say I do an ok job of it. I mostly wear pants, of course, being kind of nonbinary and all. I try to act with tzedakah, too. Or at least write with it. I used to call my Stepdad a shikker, or a drunk, sometimes. That wasn't completely fair. My Stepdad only drinks non-alcoholic beer. He's a huge fan, but you can't really call him a shikker if he never gets drunk. It's always a simcha when I come home for summer, because despite everything I've written here, I really love my family.

On the psych ward, I thought shit was holier than shema. Now I think they're about equal. I think the saying, "Oh shit!" is a very valuable one, and something we don't say often enough. I hope my family reads this and says that. My whole mishpocheh. Mameh is Mom in Yiddish, and in Hebrew it's Imah. My best friend in middle school (or best school friend, I went to school part time), once told me, "Your Imah is here" when my Mom came to pick me up. I have an unofficially adopted zun (son). There is only one person on this earth I would call a nafka, and that is my second girlfriend. Even she had a tragic backstory. Nafka means streetwalker by the way. Our relationship was drecky because she couldn't accept me as I was. My Mom sometimes wishes she could have had a shadchen, but she is currently very happy single. I will admit I had a lot of chutzpah to ever think I was the Messiah. I still have that chutzpah. I am a believer in G-d, but an apikoros to pretty much everything else supernatural.

L'chayim!

If you are interested in joining my email list, where I will send you all kinds of interesting goodies, email me at <u>alexandraberrocal@gmail.com</u> and I will add you.

If you are interested in my Patreon (where you can help financially support me so I can make more art), it can be found here: <u>www.patreon.com/alexandraberrocal</u>

And of course, visit my website at <u>deadonthevergeofblooming.wordpress.com</u>

Enjoy!